T0378911

Civic Skills and Values

Perseverance

By Dalton Rains

www.littlebluehousebooks.com

Little Blue House is distributed by North Star Editions:
sales@northstareditions.com | 888-417-0195

Produced for Little Blue House by Red Line Editorial.

Photographs ©: Shutterstock Images, cover, 4, 7, 9, 11, 12, 15, 17, 21, 23, 24 (top left), 24 (top right), 24 (bottom left), 24 (bottom right); iStockphoto, 18

Library of Congress Control Number: 2022919843

ISBN
978-1-64619-819-1 (hardcover)
978-1-64619-848-1 (paperback)
978-1-64619-904-4 (ebook pdf)
978-1-64619-877-1 (hosted ebook)

Printed in the United States of America
Mankato, MN
082023

About the Author

Dalton Rains writes and edits nonfiction children's books. He lives in Minnesota.

Table of Contents

What It Is

Perseverance means you keep on trying even when something is hard.

You might want to stop, but you keep going.

Learning new skills takes perseverance. You might fall off your bike the first time you try.

You play the wrong keys
on the piano.
Then you might want to
give up.

piano

9

Perseverance means you keep trying.
With more practice, you can learn new songs.

Struggles

Perseverance is not easy.

You might feel tired or bored.

You might not want to do your homework.

You might feel angry
when you cannot
do something.
It is hard to learn
new things.

You might feel scared
to fail.
It can be scary to mess
up in front of others.

Keep Trying

Everyone makes mistakes.

But you can learn from
your mistakes.

You can ask for help.

You might try your best and still fail.
But if you keep trying, you can succeed.

Perseverance helps
you keep going when it
is hard.
You can do hard things.

Glossary

bike

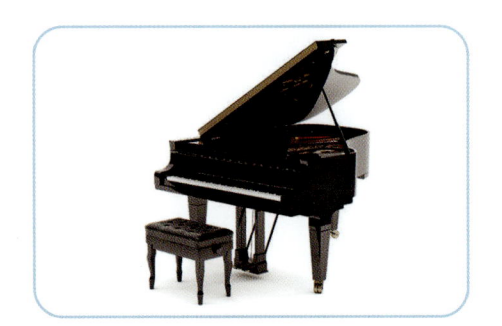
piano

homework

tired

Index